Uncage My Brave:
Pray Brave, Fly Free

By
Sara Brunsvold

ISBN: 1545234051
ISBN-13: 978-1545234051

In honor of:
God, the cage breaker
and
His Word, the feathers of my wings

Preflight Journal >>

ARE YOU IN THAT PLACE where your heart is stirred toward something but fear keeps your wings tucked in and your feet on the ground? Do you have a dream that won't go away but you are unsure if it is from God or yourself?

I know a thing or two about wanting something so badly but also fearing my choices did not align with God's will.

I have struggled to identify the difference between selfish ambition and the liberty to bravely pursue the work God has earmarked for my unique abilities. I was once afraid to even talk to God about the specific thing on my heart.

Through this struggle, I learned to pray with courage. Slowly I began to understand how to balance fear with brave, and why it is so necessary to do so.

A freedom exists when God is on our side, when we dream His dreams and soar on the air He slides under our wings. When we are of the same mind as Him, nothing, no thing, can keep us grounded. The sky opens to a rich, warm, welcome blue.

Soaring with God takes a courage much greater than our own. Courage that, like the heart's desire itself, must flow from Him.

So how does this happen? How do we know we are aligned with Him?

Through prayer. Through intimate, unreserved conversation with Him. By daily and humbly approaching the foot of His throne.

Friend, I believe you were meant to read the 12 prayers in this book. I believe He wants to speak to you through them.

These prayers are modeled after the ones I used in seeking God for wisdom and courage.

May these prayers:

>> Encourage you to be honest, specific and -- most important -- *receptive* toward God. He may have a different idea about what you really need, and though that may sound scary, I promise you His ideas are worlds better than what you can imagine.

>> Illustrate that brave is something that does not come easily nor consistently. There are ups and downs, good days and bad days. Where you are right this second does not matter as much as where God leads you over the long term.

>> Provide an example of how prayer does not have to be perfect or "conventional"; it just needs to be. None of my prayers are identical to each other, and that's okay.

If you need prayer support as you uncage your brave, I would be pleased to be on your side.

Contact me at www.SaraBrunsvold.com.

Joyful flight.

The Prayers >>

When Brave Looks Ordinary

THE STORY BEHIND THE PRAYER:

I didn't understand brave. I saw a Facebook post raving about the indominable courage of a soldier who was killed in action in Afghanistan. Reading the post, I told myself, "If that's what brave is, I'm nowhere close." I thought since I have not done or experienced anything dramatically scary, I did not qualify for bravery. As if God, during the distribution of courage, looked at me and said, "No, child, you're too weak of heart." But God, gently, turned my head another direction.

THE PRAYER:

Lord, today I struggle to believe I could possibly possess bravery.

"No, not me," I say. "I am less than the least. I am just ordinary." The world is too quick to affirm this deception for me.

The world says brave is the soldier on a wall. Brave is a patient hooked up to the chemo pump. Brave is the firefighter running back into the burning building.

I am none of these things. So how could I be brave? How do I believe brave could possibly exist inside me?

I look to the Word for examples of brave, and again I see the extraordinary: a boy facing a giant, a man with a stick parting the sea.

But, Lord, I see something else.

Brave, quite often, looked ordinary.

A woman choosing to have a baby. A king rebuilding the temple. A bleeding woman touching the hem of the Messiah's garment.

In these examples, I see a truth I have denied:

Brave lives in ordinary moments as much as it does in the *extra*ordinary.

Brave is seen in any choice to push beyond the comfortable.

Like a little girl walking into school by herself for the first time. A mom setting out clothes for her first day back from maternity leave.

Brave is the daughter-in-law prepping her first Thanksgiving turkey. It is the man who finally makes the doctor's appointment.

Brave is the husband who brings ice cream and an apology. It is the teen who stood up when everyone else was tearing down.

Brave is the parents sitting down their kid to have "the talk." It is the widower moving out of his home of 35 years.

Brave is the dad teaching his son to drive. It is the student choosing the hardest professor.

Brave is the single mom enrolling in night classes. It is the co-worker sharing her testimony over lunch.

Brave is the stranger offering his spare change. It is the son extending forgiveness long overdue.

When brave looks ordinary, it is no less special, no less praiseworthy and lovely. Brave that looks ordinary can be dangerous -- because it slips right past the enemy lines. Subtle and potent.

It quietly builds, creating a storehouse of courage.

Ordinary is the most subversive kind of brave.

Lord, today, show me the quiet brave within me, the strength You have hidden in me.

Lord, today, help me live that brave, to build on it in preparation for the extraordinary.

Help me be subversively brave against the enemy.

In Jesus' name,

Amen

Trapped

THE STORY BEHIND THE PRAYER:

God can use the lives of others as a sort of mirror to our own. Various people had come to me with prayer requests rooted in one sentiment: feeling trapped. Whether in a health situation or the effects of a poor decision or a circumstance beyond their control. Though they didn't know it, I felt the same way and didn't express it. I felt trapped in a place so far away from my dream of being a full-fledged writer. No matter what I tried, I didn't seem to move forward. As I prayed for my loved ones, I knew I needed to also acknowledge my own frustration before God.

THE PRAYER:

Trapped. That's how I feel, God.

Right where I am, in the middle of the chaos and discomfort wreaking havoc on my soul.

This feels isolating, frustrating. I feel helpless.

But You are a God who defends the defenseless (Psalm 72:12). You are a God of forward motion, in Your own time.

And I have known You to keep this promise. I have seen You do it.

The times I have felt trapped were invariably followed by the times I felt most free.

When I was trapped in loneliness as a young single, that loneliness came to a crescendo right before I unexpectedly met the man who would become my husband.

When I felt trapped in a job and had several other career doors open only to slam in my face, I was mere months away from the best career change I have ever made.

When I have felt the most hopeless, it was right before You did crazy cool stuff in my life. Sometimes You did move me from the situation, other times I lingered. Always You worked to change my perspective and my attitude, which can be just as immensely liberating as physical movement.

Being trapped has been a precursor to soul-rejuvenating freedom.

Invariably.

Almost as if I hadn't been trapped so much
as held in place by Your hand, protecting
me from outside entities that would hurt
me worse than I could imagine.

Had I succumbed to my loneliness as a
young single and desperately settled for
the company of any man I could find, I
may not have met my husband.

Had I given into the frustration of being
trapped in a job that clearly wasn't
working out and left my employer with
pride high, I may have settled for less than
what You had planned for me the entire
time.

Had I not felt trapped, I would have missed
the opportunity to witness You work.

I would have not come out of it with deep
empathy for others going through the same
thing, and a desire to pray for them. I
would not now reflect back and marvel at
how Your plan for my life has unfolded.

Although I don't know why I cannot yet
move beyond this discomfort, I do know
You do not waste any opportunity.

You are a God of forward motion.

Move me in Your timing. Grant me the
longsuffering I need to wait out Your

action. Because, wow, what a testimony I will have!

In Jesus' name,

Amen

Releasing the Death Grip

THE STORY BEHIND THE PRAYER:

The waiting game is not one I'm skilled at. This was written the week I left a job without having another to go to. Though in my heart I felt a conviction that God was leading me to a part-time job that would allow me to continue to build on my writing dream, the question mark hanging over my family was heavy. So heavy my mind began to wonder if I had made the right choice.

THE PRAYER

Is this the right path, Father? Is what I dream from You? I so badly want to know.

You know me wholly. You know I'm a planner. I'm the mom who has kids' birthday parties planned months in advance. I rarely go to the store without checking for coupons and deals. This is who I am.

So for me to think of walking away from one season of my life and not know which season is next is, well, TERRIFYING.

But, God, above wanting to know what's next, I want to lose my death grip on the future. Finger by white-knuckled finger, peel off my hand and replace it with Yours.

May I let go and be at peace with it. Peace, as in the waters may be raging but I'm snoring in the boat (Matthew 8:24). Peace.

Your plan is frequently better and bigger, and therefore nothing like mine. I realize if I'm going to follow a reliable plan, I'd be better off following one that has existed before the formation of the planet. That seems like a solid bet.

In Your grace, I know You appreciate that trusting You is a process for me.

It requires me to be still. Two of the hardest words ever for a planner: be still. We planners equate still with lazy. We tend to confuse giving it up to You with giving up. Giving up and lazy, to us, are the badges of failure and shame.

To be still is to take a huge risk.

Lord, help me to take it. Help me to be still physically. To stop trying to accomplish on my own. Stop hunting for answers in anything but Your Word. To take my fingers off the keyboard, my hand off the mouse. Let man's answers languish on the cyber vine.

Lord, help me be still emotionally, to let go of the worry and fear and doubt about tomorrow. I visualize myself laying down my emotions before You, and see how small they are compared to You!

Lord, help me be still spiritually, forever quietly and submissively before You. To allow me to LISTEN to what You are trying to say. No more talking *over* You or *for* You.

You have never failed to answer any prayer I have raised to You previously, though sometimes the answer was not what I hoped for. You have never failed to pick up on those things my heart asked but my mouth did not, and You answered those requests as well.

There is none like You (Psalm 86:8). There is none more wise and comforting. I long to hear Your voice. I want what You want in my life.

God, I have no clue what comes next, but I have no doubt You will show me. I stand ready.

In Jesus' name,

Amen

The Courage to Be Still

THE STORY BEHIND THE PRAYER:

Hands-down, one of the most powerful prayers I've ever written. By nature I am a planner, a thinker, a doer. So this...this was a hard prayer to pray. I was in a season of waiting on God and wanting to do something to speed things up, or at least feel productive. But God, in His infinite and incomparable wisdom, told me something very different in my quiet time with Him one morning.

THE PRAYER:

I want the courage to be still (Psalm 46:10), to not be afraid to exist in the spot I am instead of racing for where I think I should be, or reaching for what I think I should have.

I want the courage to shed the should's. I want the courage to not be in control, to not set the timetable, to not pick the direction, to not trust self before You.

I want the courage to fall in.

I want the courage to be open, to be here, to be present, to breathe it in. I want the courage to listen.

I want the courage to accept that stillness is not the same as laziness, that sometimes quality is not found in productivity.

I want the courage to respect I am a part of Your plan and my plans will likely fall apart.

I want the courage to be still in this time, in this place, for this purpose, to know You move even if I don't.

I want the courage to not push myself but instead let You carry me; I would arrive less worn and with impeccable timing.

I want the courage to believe there are times I must do Your will by *not doing a thing.*

Carry me, Abba. Hold me still in Your strength. Press my ear to Your heart.

Give me the courage to hear this is the start of something lovely.

In Jesus' name,

Amen

The Lie of Insignificance

THE STORY BEHIND THE PRAYER:

Writing is a tricky thing. I don't write for the attention, yet I am grieved when my work doesn't get attention. At the time I prayed this, I was looking at other, more successful writers with jealousy burning away at my soul. Jealousy, which stems from pride, is a dangerous thing to entertain. I went to God, and listened.

THE PRAYER:

DO YOU SEE ME, GOD? Wishing I was better? Greater? More significant in Your eyes? Desperate to add value? Convinced I should be something and believing I am not?

My dreams fade with each day. They are replaced by a mantra with ever-increasing volume: "You will never be. You will never do. You will never have."

This mantra casts shade on my goals, inch by inch.

"You will never be. You will never do. You will never have."

Do you see me?

Me, in a lonely room, longing for it to be filled with my greatest desire?

Me, bent with the weight of growing hopelessness?

Me, striving and yet feeling like I'm not moving at all?

You tell me repeatedly in Your Word You know me and You are with me.

Help me believe it.

Remind me, Father, that those words I am using -- better, greater, more -- exist only for the sake of comparison, for the sake of devaluing something in favor of something else.

Only one thing results from comparisons: persistent dissatisfaction.

Comparisons are fruitless.

You made me to be me, not anyone else.

You made me to do what only I can do.

If You made me to do and be and live a life You gave only to me, then I cannot compare. I cannot truly live and compare at the same time.

Tell me again comparisons are fruitless.

And if they are fruitless, then the mantra I'm hearing is all me, the worldly me, the part that yet needs to die to the power of Christ.

The part that needs to be replaced with the truth that I have a significance in this world that no one else will fulfill. No one else has the gifts, resources, life circumstance You have invested in me.

You would not spend time designing this life of mine if You did not also intend for me to use it. You would not invest in the details of me if they had no consequence. No. You don't do inconsequential.

Help me disbelieve the lies, Lord, and fall headlong into the freedom of knowing You do not see me as less.

You see me as beautiful.

You see me as capable and mighty with the strength of the Spirit.

Lord, help me believe it.

In Jesus' name,

Amen

Lord, I Can't Hear You

THE STORY BEHIND THE PRAYER:

Sometimes God is abundantly clear which way He wants us to go. Other times, He is not so clear. I was in the latter, unsure what my next job was going to be or even if I could find one. Multiple possibilities lay in front of me, and I was unsure which one was right. I wanted Him to be more vocal, more apparent about where He was leading me. He needed me to remember to trust.

THE PRAYER:

Lord, I am asking You: Where do I go from here? Which way do I turn? I am standing at this fork in the road and everything is blank. I cannot tell which path is Yours. My feet are trembling. My mind is spinning.

My ears clamor to hear a voice behind me saying "This is the way, walk in it" (Isaiah 30:21). Lord, do I turn right or left? Do I boldly go through the middle of this, or do I quietly go around? I am straining to hear You. To find Your voice over all the others. I am desperate to hear it.

I need You to speak. To move me, to guide me — to *shove* me — in the direction I need to go. I'm OK with a whisper. I'm OK with a shout. So long as You speak. Don't let me go astray. Don't let me wander down the wrong path. Don't let me be fooled into believing another voice is Yours.

I have tried to speak for You before, and I have always given myself the wrong directions.

I need to hear You, because I will lead myself astray. A sheep cannot be its own shepherd.

Am I so far away from You that I can't hear You? Are You so far away from me that I can't make out what You're saying? Are my own fears, worries, anxieties, wants blocking You out?

Lord, I can't hear You. Please unlock Yourself from this silence. Let the voice I love ring in my ear. What is it You will say? What is it You want me to hear?

Let me hear what God the Lord will say, for You will speak peace to me (Psalm 85:8).

Tell me the great and hidden things I do not know (Jeremiah 33:3).

Remember me here at this fork and do not withhold Your words. Speak above the noise. Speak directly into me.

My wisdom comes from You, and what I lack in it now, please give generously without reservation (James 1:5).

Lord, I wait. And I listen.

In Jesus' name,

Amen

Because What's Ahead is so Unclear

THE STORY BEHIND THE PRAYER:

This was written almost a year after "Lord, I Can't Hear You." It's amazing how quickly we fall back into our flesh ways and forget God is worth our trust. Though He had faithfully led me to a new job that does allow me to pursue my writing dream, I was experiencing a number of road blocks in writing and had fallen into discouragement. I wondered if writing truly was the right pursuit. I struggled to find the words to express my heart. The beautiful thing about God is He *gives us the words* to pray. I drew heavily on the prayers of Biblical dream chasers.

THE PRAYER:

God, I need You. Because what's ahead is so unclear. I am frustrated. I am worried. I am awake with anxiety.

I strain to see what's next. I labor to make out something. *Anything.*

If I only knew, I would be at peace.

All I see is gray—uninterpretable and formless.

If only I knew.

I groan under the weight of not knowing.

I want to believe whatever awaits beyond the gray is good, because You are good (Psalm 34:8).

I want to believe You have surrounded me with Your angels (Psalm 37:4) and that You are at the forward most point.

Teach me to believe, Lord.

Remind me how wide and long and deep and tall is Your goodness (Ephesians 3:18).

Remind me the plans You have specially chosen for me will bring me hope and a future (Jeremiah 29:11).

In my frustration, strengthen me to stand firm and see the deliverance You will give me (Exodus 14:13).

In my worry, remind me You have already seen tomorrow. Remind me of the steps You led me along yesterday, and that You are the same God who walked with me then – the very same. You never change (Malachi 3:6).

You will shine a bright lamp for my feet and make my path straight and clear in perfect time (Psalm 119:105).

You still the hunger of those You cherish (Psalm 107:9).

If I should begin to lose faith and be tempted to stall where I am or romanticize where I was, tell me to follow. Tell me to go. What awaits is immeasurably more than I could ask or imagine (Ephesians 3:20).

Surely I will never be shaken. I will have no fear because my heart is steadfast, trusting in You (Psalm 112:6-7). In the end, I will look in triumph over my anxious thoughts because You have told me I am more than a conqueror (Romans 8:37).

I will say with confidence the Lord is my helper (Hebrews 13:6).

Many alternative plans battle within my heart, but Your purpose, Lord, prevails (Proverbs 19:21). I lay my plans down, cast them to the gutter. I want Yours.

It is in who You are, rather than my circumstance, I find my peace.

Guide me and teach me, because what's ahead is so unclear.

In Jesus' name,

Amen

I Want *that* Kind of Faith

THE STORY BEHIND THE PRAYER:

In a Bible study at church, we were looking at the life of Elijah, specifically the point where God, to save Elijah's life, sends him to a remote area. God tells Elijah to wait by a freshwater brook and eat whatever ravens bring him. The astounding thing? Elijah did it. At the time we studied this passage, I wanted to be stronger in my faith, stronger in my conviction that God was on my side, stronger in my belief that God *was* asking me to go and wait and be still as He worked on my behalf in writing. I wanted Elijah's kind of faith.

THE PRAYER:

I don't want just any old faith, Heavenly Father. I want a *rock star* faith. I want the kind of faith Elijah had when God told him to leave the dangerous world he knew, go hide by a remote brook and rely on ravens to bring him food (1 Kings 17:1-6).

How much courage does it require to believe a bird — a *filthy scavenger* at that

— would actually bring you food that you would actually eat? That is rock star faith.

I want that kind of faith.

I want the kind of faith that responds to "Leave here" with feet running. I want the kind of faith that doesn't ask why, how, "You mean right now" or "are You sure it's me"? I want the kind of faith that takes me to the life above.

I want the kind of faith that puts me so near to You, my Creator, that I have no doubt when You are speaking to me.

The kind of faith that has the courage to go instead of standing frozen in fearful thoughts. The kind of faith that takes me to an unknown place where I have only to *be*, where my circumstances are 100% out of my hands, where I can't even find food myself.

I want the kind of faith that keeps me still, knowing You are God (Psalm 46:10) and expecting You to act as such.

I want the kind of faith that lives on as a legacy for generations. I want that kind of faith.

I want it even though it's scary to ask for it because You will undoubtedly say yes. Then You will use it, call me into the deep.

Because faith comes with a call to lean on it.

As scary as it may be, I ask for that kind of faith, because what better weapon is there against fear?

A faith that strikes harder than fear --
that's the faith I want.

Lord, may it grow within me.

In Jesus' name,

Amen

If You Move Me from This Place

THE STORY BEHIND THE PRAYER:

When it became apparent God was leading me into unexplored territory with writing, I began to seize with fear. What if I can't do this? What if I'm not good enough? What if I fail? Fear had convinced me I was comfortable where I was and didn't really want to move. Fear had threatened to thwart the very thing I had asked God to do: to move me from the place I felt trapped. The best way to overcome fear is to face it head-on. That is what I did in this prayer.

THE PRAYER:

Lord, I feel You calling me away from this place. And it scares me. I am terrified.

I know this place. It is comfortable to me. But out there? I'm not sure I'm cut out for it. I used to think maybe I was, back when it was just a girl with a silly dream that One Day Oh One Day.

I feel You moving me. Lord, are You sure? Can You assure me this is right?

Will You please send me a sign that I am hearing You right? Is that wrong to ask of You? If it's wrong, then I'm already in the wrong, so what's the harm in asking again. Lord, will You?

Not knowing is driving me crazy. Don't let me descend into the pit of doubt and fear. Let me feel my wings. Let me see my feathers. Let me know I am ready to be nudged from this nest.

Lord, if You move me from this place, please walk with me. Please hold my hand. Please let me hide behind Your legs when we get there, at least for a bit.

You tell me, "Be brave, child." I will be brave if You are my shield. My sword. My armor. That's the only way brave is ever going to happen. Make my shield so form-fitting fear can't slip in.

It's more than fear I feel. I also feel sadness.

Lord, if You move me from this place, my heart will ache for what I leave behind. It will ache for the things that will look different or not exist at all where I'm going. These are the things I will miss the most. These things I did not recognize as the lovely until I began to feel You say, "It's almost time to go."

Let me linger just a bit longer. Not forever. Long enough to pin these moments in my memory. Long enough to look at this place in a new way, a way that brings light to the treasures and glory to You.

Look at them with me, will You? Tell me, "Yes, I put those there for you to enjoy. Did you like them?" Then I will reply, "Very much. Oh, very much."

And You will say, "Wait until you see what's next."

I know You will be speaking the truth, a promise You intend to keep. You have never moved me to a place without something waiting for me. You have been faithful. You work for my good; not to harm me, but to propel me.

You would not nudge me from this nest unless You knew I could fly.

No.

So, hold my hand, Lord. Lead me. I will follow, spreading my wings along the way.

In Jesus' name,

Amen

Make Me a Risker

THE STORY BEHIND THE PRAYER:

God can use His Word to awaken in us a desire we need in order for Him to accomplish His plan in our lives. This is what happened here. In God's perfect timing, He gave me biblical examples of people who left behind what they knew and headed into the unknown when He called them, despite the risks. Because He is worth the risk. These examples awoke in me a desire to follow their lead, and His prompting.

THE PRAYER:

Lord, make me a risker.

Help me leave my nets on the ground and follow where I have not yet been (Matthew 4:20).

Lord, make me a risker who braves the hard and the hurt to arrive where beautiful lives.

A risker who believes when I do not know, and trusts when I cannot plan.

A risker whose ear is trained on only You, and whose eyes see past what's directly in front of me.

Lord, make me a risker who disbelieves naysayers, who fears not the schemes of man (Psalm 37:7), or the criticism of those too scared to try.

Whose strategy does not include worry over things uncontrollable but focus on what is to be learned.

A risker who heads toward the unknown like it is a friend yet to be made.

Let me give in to the prompting of the still small voice (1 Kings 19:12).

Let me *not* give in to the temptation to second guess.

Lord, make me a risker unwilling to waver.

In Jesus' name,

Amen

Your Voice Be Louder

THE STORY BEHIND THE PRAYER:

This was originally written for my daughter. Sensitive little heart that she is, she needs extra encouragement sometimes, and I wanted her to grasp just how boldly she can walk knowing the Lord walks with her. As I wrote, God opened my eyes to how my own boldness had grown, the cage on my brave had opened. In no small thanks to the extra encouragement He had given me countless times.

THE PRAYER:

Here I am again, in a new place, Lord. A new phase. A new challenge.

And I am happy...and scared.

In the middle of the joy this brings, I hear a voice in my head I know all too well. The one that questions what I am capable of, what I am worthy of and what I could possibly offer this world.

Lord, I pray I do not listen to this voice. It is the ugliest, meanest, stinkiest voice.

I will never know what I am capable of, I will never know my full worth, I will never know the vastness of what I have to offer this world by listening to that voice.

I will only know these things by listening to You.

And I hear You say I can make mistakes. No experience will stretch me like mistakes will. No lesson strikes harder. So may I own my mistakes, seek forgiveness for them at the moment I need to.

I hear You say seek the lovely (Philippians 4:8). You say I am worthy of nothing less than selfless friendship, encouraging words, and healthy affection. I will not settle for anyone offering me less because such peddlers are but wilting flowers.

I hear You say be the lovely. You have created me wholly and uniquely (Psalm 139:14). Because of You, I offer this world something it needs.

Father God, be the louder voice.

Help me not allow any other voice to drown out Your beautiful, life-giving words.

In Jesus' name,

Amen

It's Time to Believe I Can

THE STORY BEHIND THE PRAYER:

My oldest was learning to ride a bike and struggled with the taking-off part. Once she began peddling, she was fine. But the starting part was hard for her. Every time, she wanted to feel and see my hand holding onto her seat, keeping her steady and sure. I would tell her repeatedly she was ready to do it on her own, but still she asked for my hand. I knew she had everything she needed, if only she believed. In the middle of this bike lesson, I heard God ask, "Do you see? Do you finally see what I've been saying?"

THE PRAYER:

How many times have I asked with a shaky voice, "God, are You holding on? Are You?"

How many times have I been terrified to get going down the path You have shown me, afraid I will fall flat on my face? How many times have I wanted You to do it for me,

labeling it "dependence on God"?
Convincing myself I am yet too weak, too
incapable?

So many times.

Which then leads to the question: how
many times have You been beside me,
hand hovering nearby, telling me to just
go? Believe, and go!

Every. Single. Time.

You were there, always, but You couldn't,
wouldn't do it for me. It had to be my
choice to move forward.

You call me to rest fully on Your hand and
believe You have equipped me to go.

I must trust You have prepared me for the
moment at hand. I must trust You have
prepared me for this choice between fear
and victory. One choice that will put my
faith into living action, a kinetic
confidence.

Dependence on You is a great thing, a vital
thing, but still *I* must move. I must trust
You have given me all I need. As I teeter on
my heels, heart thumping and mind
racing, will I trust Your hand hovers
nearby, a safety net, but not a prop?

The choice is mine to make. The steps are
mine to take. If it's victory in Christ I am

after, then at some point, I have to start. I have to step.

You believe I can, You know I can, and better still — You have already seen me do it.

You will never leave. You will never take Your eyes off me. But You wait for me to decide.

I choose to step. Be my guide, Lord.

In Jesus' name,

Amen

BONUS MATERIAL

QUOTES AND SCRIPTURE TO ENCOURAGE YOU

1.   "Go confidently in the direction of your dreams. Live the life you've imagined."
       >> Henry David Thoreau

2.   "Remember to celebrate milestones as you prepare for the road ahead."
       >> Nelson Mandela

3.   "As soon as you start to pursue your dream, your life wakes up and everything has meaning."
       >> Barbara Sher

4.   "You are never too old to set another goal or to dream a new dream."
       >> C.S. Lewis

5.   "The person with big dreams is more powerful than the one with all the facts."
       >> Albert Einstein

6.   "I will instruct you and teach you in the way you should go; I will counsel you with my loving eye on you."
       >> Psalm 32:8

7. "Twenty years from now you will be more disappointed by the things that you didn't do than by the ones you did do. So throw off the bowlines. Sail away from the safe harbor. Catch the trade winds in your sails. Explore. Dream. Discover."
>> Mark Twain

8. "Every great dream begins with a dreamer. Always remember, you have within you the strength, the patience, and the passion to reach for the stars to change the world."
>> Harriet Tubman

9. "There is nothing like a dream to create the future."
>> Victor Hugo

10. "Let the current of your being set toward God, then your life will be filled and calmed by one master-passion which unites and stills the soul."
>> Alexander MacLaren

11. "The soul without imagination is what an observatory would be without a telescope."
>> Henry Ward Beecher

12. "God is more interested in your future and your relationships than you are."
>> Billy Graham

13. "When I'm old and dying, I plan to look back on my life and say, 'Wow, that was an adventure,' not, 'Wow, I sure felt safe.'"
>> Tom Preston-Werner

14. "The way of the dreamer is difficult, but anything less is hardly living at all."
>> Bruce Wilkinson

15. "Commit your work to the Lord, and your plans will be established."
>> Proverbs 16:3

16. "But seek first the kingdom of God and his righteousness, and all these things will be added to you."
>> Matthew 6:33

PRACTICAL STEPS TO UNCAGE YOUR BRAVE

Prayer is essential to freeing the power God has planted inside of you to pursue the plans He has for you. At some point, though, it is also essential to move based on prayer.

Here are practical steps to take, one by one, each building on the last.

1. Find a quiet, private place daily to talk openly with God about what is on your heart. Do not be afraid about offending him. Just talk, candidly. Then, LISTEN to what he says. Be open to what he says. Seek answers in Scripture.

2. After careful prayer, write a vision statement describing what your dream is and commit it to memory. Ask God for a Scripture verse to tie to your vision statement, and commit that verse to memory as well.

3. Share your full, uncensored dream and vision with at least two reliable prayer warriors. These should be godly people you trust and know well. Ask them for prayer support as you pursue the vision God has given you. Provide regular updates so they know how to specifically pray in unison with you.

4. Find a godly accountability partner who will push you to pursue your vision. This may or may not be one of the people offering prayer support. It's wise to choose someone who understands what it takes to fulfill your vision, if such a person is within your circle. It's most effective to choose someone whose style best fits your needs. For instance, if you need someone who is not afraid to get tough, then go for someone with such a personality. Also, be specific with your partner about how and to what exactly you want them to hold you accountable. For example, do you want daily reminders? Do you want someone who requests to see proof of work each week?

5. Begin to dedicate at least 10 minutes of *action* time most days of the week toward your dream. Action means making meaningful strides toward your vision, whether that is conducting research, meeting with strategic partners or experts, producing something of value, etc. Action time is outside of daily prayer time. Work with your accountability partner if necessary to define "meaningful."

PARTING NOTE

Brave one,

I can see you taking flight already. Pray, seek and do not fear. He is with you and has already watched you soar.

I speak from personal experience when I say brave is yours for the taking.

Thank you for reading, and if I can offer prayers for you in your journey, please send me a note through my blog, www.SaraBrunsvold.com.

One last thing before we part: I ask you to remember this book and its contents represent my soul and hard work. Please do not distribute this book or any of its contents without my consent. Ask me, and I will gladly work with you on an alternative solution.

Blessings and bravery to you,

Sara

About the author:

Sara Brunsvold is a lifelong dream chaser and a more recent brave acquirer. She now writes, ministers and loves more fully and courageously knowing God's plan is the only one worth her life.

She lives in the Kansas City area with her husband, two daughters, one small dog and her laptop.

Connect with her at www.SaraBrunsvold.com.

Made in the USA
Middletown, DE
23 June 2017